Wild About Wheels

BREAKDOWN TRUCKS

Nancy Dickmann

raintree
a Capstone company — publishers for children

Raintree is an imprint of Capstone Global Library Limited, a company incorporated in England and Wales having its registered office at 264 Banbury Road, Oxford, OX2 7DY – Registered company number: 6695582

www.raintree.co.uk
myorders@raintree.co.uk

Hardback edition © Capstone Global Library Limited 2022
Paperback edition © Capstone Global Library Limited 2023
The moral rights of the proprietor have been asserted.

All rights reserved. No part of this publication may be reproduced in any form or by any means (including photocopying or storing it in any medium by electronic means and whether or not transiently or incidentally to some other use of this publication) without the written permission of the copyright owner, except in accordance with the provisions of the Copyright, Designs and Patents Act 1988 or under the terms of a licence issued by the Copyright Licensing Agency, 5th Floor, Shackleton House, 4 Battle Bridge Lane, London SE1 2HX (www.cla.co.uk). Applications for the copyright owner's written permission should be addressed to the publisher.

Edited by Amy McDonald Maranville
Designed by Cynthia Della-Rovere
Original illustrations © Capstone Global Library Limited 2022
Picture research by Eric Gohl
Production by Katy LaVigne
Originated by Capstone Global Library Ltd
Printed and bound in India

978 1 3982 2460 5 (hardback)
978 1 3982 2459 9 (paperback)

British Library Cataloguing in Publication Data
A full catalogue record for this book is available from the British Library.

Acknowledgements
We would like to thank the following for permission to reproduce photographs:
Alamy: Jeppe Gustafsson, 7, Naude/Dave.J.Smith, 11; Capstone Studio: Karon Dubke, 5, 9, 17, 21 (art supplies); Getty Images: DarrenMower, 15, Helena Wahlman, 8, 13; iStockphoto: kozmoat98, 6, 18–19, ThamKC, 16; Shutterstock: aapsky, 4, Labrador Photo Video, 14, New Africa, 12, Red Orange, 21 (drawing), Sophie Grukhina (background), throughout, ThamKC, cover, Vitpho, 10

Every effort has been made to contact copyright holders of material reproduced in this book. Any omissions will be rectified in subsequent printings if notice is given to the publisher.

All the internet addresses (URLs) given in this book were valid at the time of going to press. However, due to the dynamic nature of the internet, some addresses may have changed, or sites may have changed or ceased to exist since publication. While the author and publisher regret any inconvenience this may cause readers, no responsibility for any such changes can be accepted by either the author or the publisher.

Contents

What breakdown trucks do 4

Look inside. 8

Look outside 10

Breakdown truck diagram . . . 18

Draw a breakdown truck 20

Glossary 22

Find out more. 23

Index 24

Words in **bold** are in the glossary.

What breakdown trucks do

A car has broken down. It won't go. And it's blocking the road! Other traffic needs to get past. It's time to call a breakdown truck!

A breakdown truck is big and strong. It uses special tools to pull the car. The truck takes the car to a garage. People at the garage can fix it.

Breakdown trucks can help when cars have been in accidents. They can pull a car out of a ditch. They can move wrecked cars. Now other cars can use the road.

Sometimes cars need to be towed at night. Breakdown trucks have warning lights. They flash so other drivers can see the lights. Now they will not hit the truck.

Look inside

A driver sits in the **cab**. The cab is at the front of the truck. There are controls there. One switch controls the warning lights. Other switches get the truck ready to tow.

Some breakdown trucks have **radios**. Breakdown company workers use radios to talk to the drivers. They tell the drivers where to find the cars that need to be towed.

Look outside

There are different types of breakdown trucks. Their parts make them look different from one another. Some breakdown trucks move buses and lorries. These tow trucks have extra wheels and **axles**. They help the trucks tow very heavy loads.

These tow trucks also have a **boom**. A boom is a type of lifting arm. It can move a big bus. It can lift a lorry out of a ditch.

Some breakdown trucks are called flatbeds. The back end is flat. It can tilt down. Now it looks like a ramp. The driver attaches a **cable** to the car. A **winch** winds it in.

The car rolls up the ramp. Then the ramp tilts back up. The driver **secures** the car. Straps are attached to the wheels. Now the truck can drive. The car will not roll off.

Some breakdown trucks have a hook and chain. It loops around a car's axle. The chain lifts up one end of the car. The other end stays on the ground.

The truck pulls the car along. This kind of towing can damage a car. It is often used on cars that are already damaged.

A wheel lift truck picks up one end of a car. But it is different from a hook and chain. It does not use chains. Instead, it has a part called a **yoke**.

The yoke slides under the car's wheels. Then the yoke lifts them up. It is quick and easy to use. It does not damage the car. Off the car goes!

Breakdown truck diagram

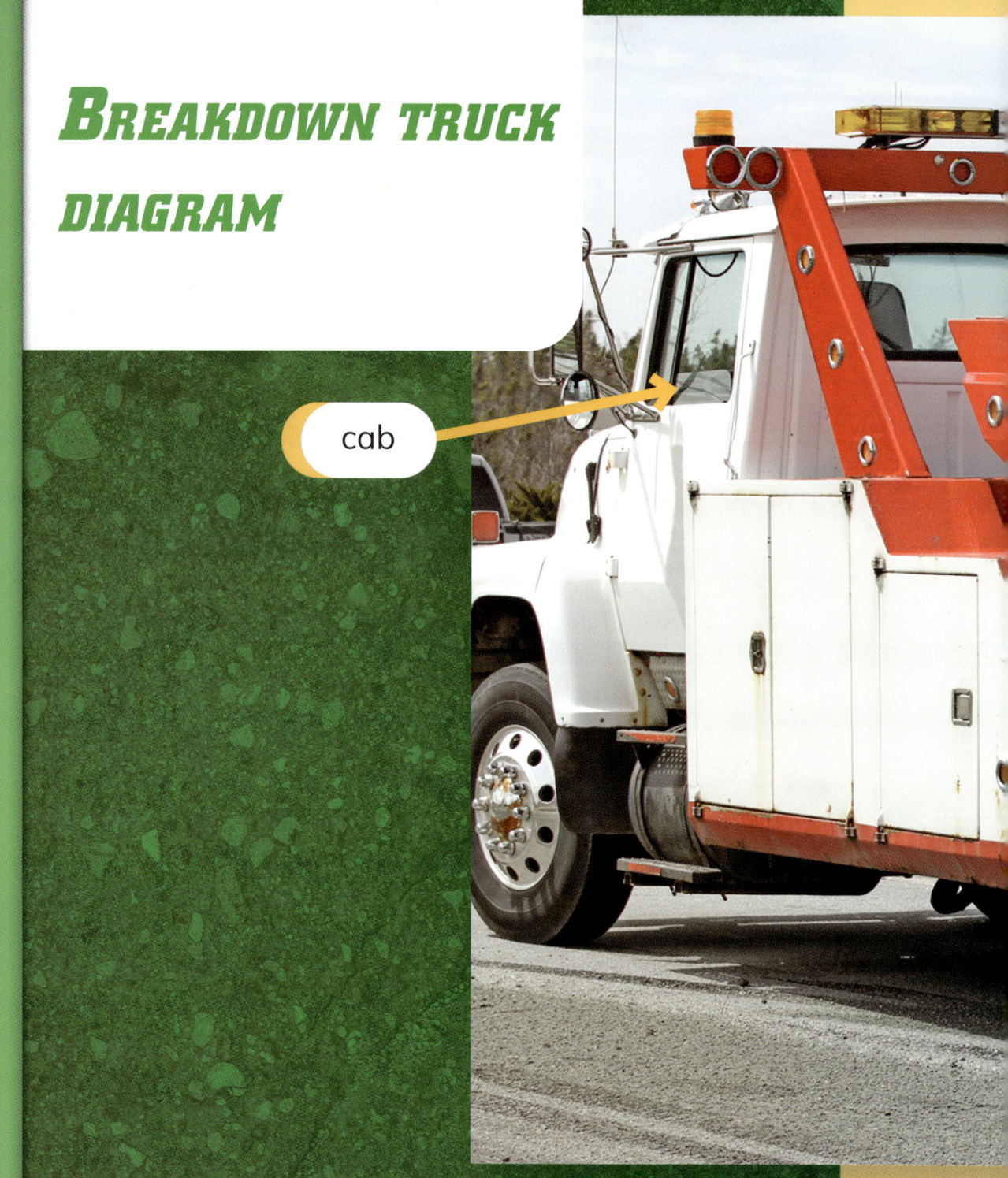

cab

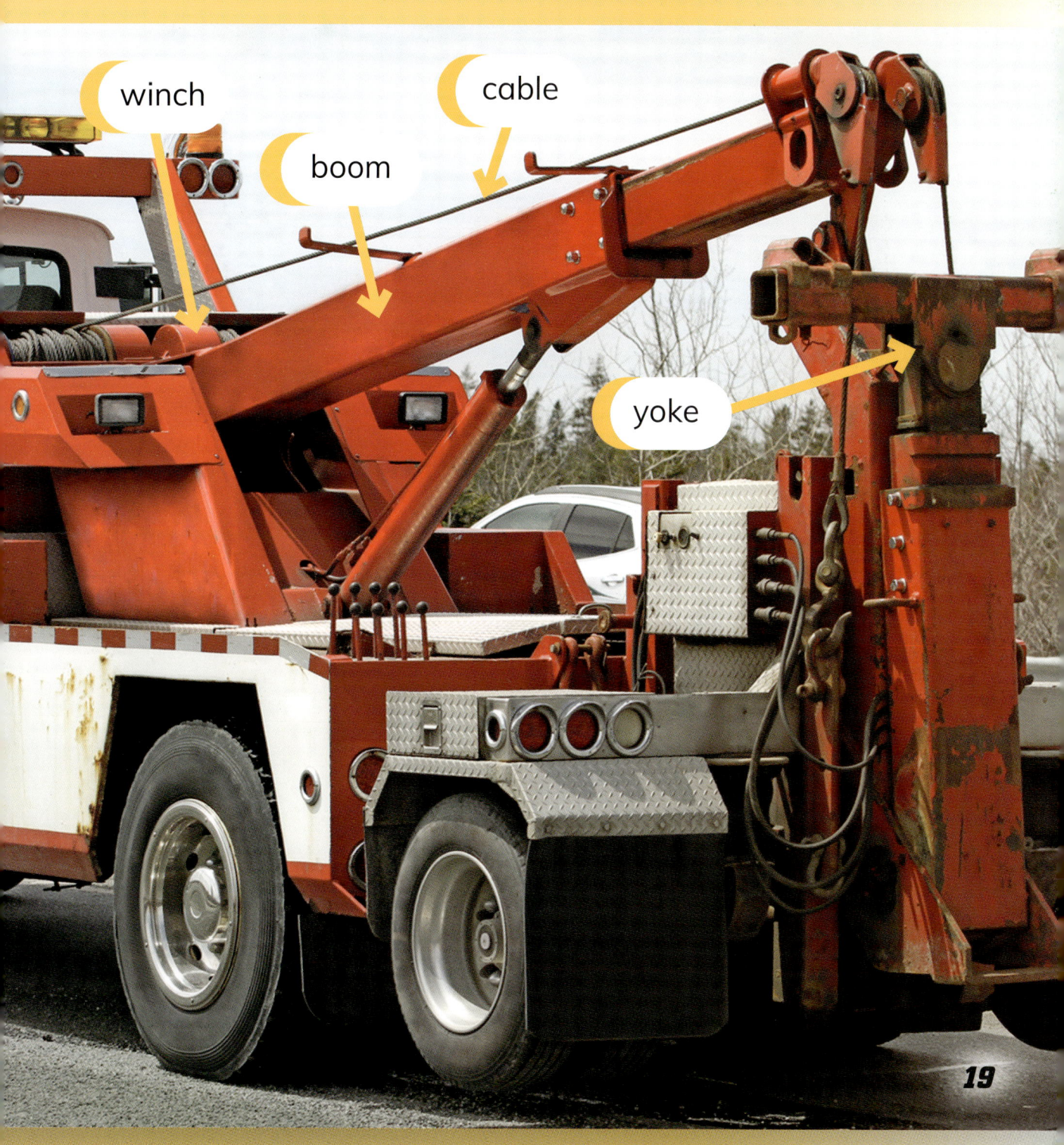

Draw a breakdown truck

What kind of breakdown truck do you like best? Draw a picture of it. How many wheels does it have? What kind of towing tools does it use? Will it have a boom? What will it be towing? Make sure you include a cab and flashing lights.

Glossary

axle strong bar with wheels at each end that spin around

boom lifting arm that extends out and can lift a heavy weight

cab compartment at the front of a vehicle, where the driver sits

cable strong rope that is often made of metal

radio device used to talk to someone far away

secure make something stable or safe

winch tool that winds a cable around a drum to pull or lift up a load

yoke metal bar on some breakdown trucks that holds a car's wheels

Find out more

Books

Emergency Rescue: Meet Real-life Heroes (DK Readers Level 3), Camilla Gersh (DK Children, 2016)

Emergency Vehicles, Simon Tyler (Faber & Faber, 2020)

Trucks and Lorries (Transport in My Community), Cari Meister (Raintree, 2020)

Website

www.bbc.co.uk/programmes/m0009p04
Watch this CBeebies show to see a breakdown truck towing a bus.

Index

accidents 6

axles 10, 14

booms 11

cabs 8

controls 8

drivers 7, 8, 9, 12, 13

flatbed tow trucks 12, 13

hooks and chains 14, 16

lights 7, 8

radios 9

repair shops 5

tools 5

traffic 4

wheel lift trucks 16

wheels 10, 17

wrecked cars 6

yokes 16, 17